W9-BSY-382

Animals That Walk on Water

ANIMALS THAT WALK ON WATER

PATRICIA A. FINK MARTIN

A First Book

Franklin Watts
A Division of Grolier Publishing
New York • London • Hong Kong • Sydney
Danbury, Connecticut

JUV. QL122.2.M37 1997

To Jerry and Leslie for their encouragement and patience

Special thanks to Brendan January for pulling this manuscript out of the editorial slush pile.

Expert reader: Kathy Carlstead, Ph.D., National Zoological Park, Washington, D.C. Illustrations created by Maud Kernan.

Photographs ©: Academy of Natural Sciences, VIREO: 25; Animals Animals: cover, 17 (Stephen Dalton), 46 (Stephen Dalton/OSF), 21 (Don Enger), 50 (OSF), 36 (Glenn Vanstrum); National Geographic Society: 38 (Bianca Lavies); North Wind Picture Archives: 14; Photo Researchers: 48 (Stephen Dalton), 8, 41 (Herman Eisenbeiss), 32, 34 (Robert Noonan), 12 (David T. Roberts), 31 (Harry Rogers), 28 (John Serrao), 39 (Kenneth H. Thomas), 15 (K.G. Vock/OKAPIA), chapter openers, 2,(David Weintraub); Visuals Unlimited: 43 (W.A. Banaszewski), 24 (Barsi), 18 (Glenn M. Oliver), 29 (John Serrao).

Library of Congress Cataloging-in-Publication Data

Martin, Patricia A. Fink, 1955–
    Animals that walk on water / Patricia A. Fink Martin
    p.   cm. — (A First book)
    Includes bibliographical references and index.
    Summary: Describes how such creatures as the basilisk, western grebe, and water strider manage to travel across the water's surface.
    ISBN 0-531-20297-6 (lib. bdg.)   ISBN 0-531-15896-9 (pbk.)
    1. Aquatic animals—Juvenile literature. 2. Animal-water relationships—Juvenile literature. 3. Animal locomotion—Juvenile literature. 4. Surface tension—Juvenile literature. [1. Aquatic animals. 2. Animal locomotion. 3. Surface tension.] I. Title. II. Series.
    QL122.2.M37   1997
    591.47'9—dc21   96-37287
                                                                                            CIP
                                                                                             AC

©1997 by Patricia A. Fink Martin
All rights reserved. Published simultaneously in Canada.
Printed in the United States of America.
1 2 3 4 5 6 7 8 9 10 R 05 04 03 02 01 00 99 98 97

CONTENTS

CHAPTER ONE

Water's Powerful Forces and Invisible Skin 9

CHAPTER TWO

A Lizard With a Dragon in Its Past: The Basilisk 13

CHAPTER THREE

Water Dancer: The Western Grebe 20

CHAPTER FOUR

An Eight-Legged Fisherman: The Fisher Spider 27

CHAPTER FIVE

Skaters With a Deadly Mission: The Water Strider 37

CHAPTER SIX
An Aquatic Pedestrian: The Water Measurer **45**

CHAPTER SEVEN
Jet Skier: The Rove Beetle **51**

GLOSSARY 56

FOR FURTHER READING 59

INDEX 61

Animals That Walk on Water

A common water strider spends most of its time resting effortlessly on the water's surface.

Water's Powerful Forces and Invisible Skin

Pour yourself a glass of water and study the surface for a minute. Now poke the tip of your finger through it. Does the surface feel hard? Does it feel slick or springy? Probably not, but to other, smaller animals that same surface does seem hard, slick, or springy.

For some animals, water is a place to walk, run, and jump. While some of these animals are as small as grains of rice, others are as large as ducks. To a small insect called the water strider, water is a shaky, fragile surface. It is a slippery, springy trampoline on which a water strider can jump or row. To the basilisk lizard, water is a thick fluid to dash across. Large or small, these animals do what we cannot.

As the larger animals run across the surface, water pushes against their feet and legs. Water pushes against any object moving through it. To feel this push or *force* for yourself, fill the bathtub with water. Make your right hand into a small paddle by bringing your fingers close together and cupping your palm slightly. Now move your hand back and forth through the water.

The push you feel against your hand is called *drag force*. Although the drag force won't support you if you try to walk or run on water, it can support the basilisk lizard and a duck-sized bird called the western grebe.

The water's surface can also support a number of insects and spiders. These smaller animals can walk, hop, row, or run on water because some of their *tissues* and other body parts are filled with air. Like a beach ball, these parts are *buoyant*.

These small creatures are also held up by water's invisible skin—a film so weak that we can't even feel it when we touch the surface. Our fingers and other heavy objects go right through it. What is this film made of? Why and how does it form? Why can't we see it? Before you can answer these questions, you must know more about water.

Water is made up of tiny bits of matter. These units of matter are called *molecules*. A single drop of water contains a sextillion (1,000,000,000,000,000,000,000) water molecules. The water molecules on the surface of water pull on each other, while other water molecules pull at them from below. As a result, the water molecules at the surface are drawn closer together. They are so close to one another that they form a skin or film.

Do you believe that water has an invisible skin or do you need proof? With only a sewing needle and a bowl of water, you can prove to yourself that the *surface film* exists. Begin by pouring some water into a cup or bowl. Next, borrow a sewing needle from your mom or dad and carefully lay it on the water's surface. The needle should remain on the surface because it is held up by the surface film.

If the needle sinks, hold it just above the water's surface and gently drop it on the water. If the needle still sinks, place a small piece of paper towel on the water and lay the needle on top of it. When the paper towel sinks, the needle should stay on the surface.

Like the needle, some small animals do not sink below the water's surface. These animals have adapted to life on the water in strange and fascinating ways. In the pages that follow you'll learn more about them. You'll also discover some of the amazing features of water!

A green-crested basilisk lizard perches on a tree branch in a jungle in Costa Rica.

CHAPTER TWO

A Lizard With a Dragon in Its Past: The Basilisk

Somewhere in a jungle in Central America, a lizard clings to a tree branch. Below, a river rushes along. The lizard grips the branch with long fingerlike toes. A thick muscular tail dangles from its body.

Eee-ee-ee-eeck! The shrill call of a circling hawk echoes through the jungle. Frightened, the lizard throws itself into the river. It hits the water with a splash and sinks to the bottom. Seconds later, it rises to the surface, and rears up on its hind legs. Then, in a spray of water, the animal sprints across the surface of the water. With its strange looks and stunning behavior, this lizard has amazed humans for centuries.

The lizard's head crest reminded European explorers of the dragons they had read about as children. These stories were written during the *Middle Ages* when most people believed that dragons actually

The legendary basilisk terrified people of the Middle Ages. The basilisk, also called the king of serpents, is pictured here with the head of a rooster and the body and tail of a serpent.

existed. These people were deathly afraid of a particular crested dragon called the basilisk. They believed that a single glance from this dragon meant certain death. Because the Central American lizard reminded the explorers of the crested dragon, they named the lizard basilisk, too.

Unlike their legendary namesake, basilisk lizards are harmless to humans. They eat ants and other small animals as well as fruits. Most basilisks are less than 24 inches (61 cm) long and live in the trees along rivers and streams.

Only the male basilisk has a head crest. But both male and female basilisks run upright. Like some small dinosaurs, these lizards run on their muscular hind legs.

The male basilisk lizard attracts females with its prominent head crest.

They move quickly on the ground, along the tree branches, and across the water's surface. Their long tail, which is held above the water, helps them balance on two legs.

The Mexicans call the basilisk the "Jesus Christ lizard" because it can run on water. Still, there is nothing supernatural about this lizard. Scientists have studied the basilisk's movement using slow-motion movie film and video photography.

These films show the lizards running through the water rather than on top of it. As they run, they sway from side to side. When young lizards run through the water, only their feet and lower legs are below the water's surface. Older, heavier lizards sink a little lower in the water.

Young or old, these lizards run swiftly across the water. First, the basilisk thrusts one foot downward through the water, producing a splash. Next, the basilisk lifts its other foot high above the water and swings it forward in a wide arc to complete the stride.

When the basilisk lizard runs on water, *Newton's third law of motion* is at work. Sir Isaac Newton, who lived from 1624–1727, was a great English scientist and mathematician. He proposed that when one object pushes on a second object, the second object pushes back. In other words, for every action, there is an equal but opposite reaction.

As the basilisk runs, each foot slaps the water's surface. The water in return pushes back. As the lizard's foot thrusts downward into the water, it pushes some water out of the

This photograph of a basilisk lizard running on water was taken with special camera equipment.

The toes on a basilisk lizard's hind feet have flaps of skin that unfold when the lizard is running on water.

way—or *displaces* the water. This creates an equal but opposite force, which pushes upward and forward. This opposing push is caused by the drag force. That force supports the lizard as it runs across the water, but why is the drag force so strong? And why can't all lizards run on water?

The basilisk's hind feet and hind legs make this lizard special. The long toes of the basilisk have a flap of skin along each side. When the lizard is on land, these flaps curl up alongside the toes. But when the animal enters the water, the flaps unfold and the feet become paddles.

Because these paddlelike feet displace more water than other types of feet, they create a greater drag force.

Speed also adds to the drag force. The faster the lizard's feet move, the greater the force produced. The basilisk's muscular hind legs propel it over the water's surface at speeds of 6 to 8 miles (10 to 13 km) per hour.

When the basilisk slows down, it drops onto all four legs and the rest of its body sinks into the water. If the lizard still feels threatened, it begins to swim.

More than 100 years have passed since explorers were first captivated by this unusual creature. In recent years, scientists have learned the secret behind the basilisk lizard's ability to run on water. Nevertheless, the basilisk continues to amaze us with its strange appearance and fascinating behavior.

CHAPTER THREE

WATER DANCER: THE WESTERN GREBE

In the spring, many waterbirds leave their winter homes. Migrating great distances, they return to their summer breeding grounds. Among them is the western grebe, a large black-and-white bird with a long, graceful neck, bold red eyes, and a dangerously pointed, yellow bill. These birds winter along the Pacific coast of the United States and Mexico. In April and May, they return to the inland waters of the western United States and Canada.

When they reach their destination, western grebes gather by the hundreds or even thousands. Hoots, piercing wails, and raspy chuckles fill the air. The sounds of water spraying and splashing mingle with their cries. It is the mating season of the western grebe.

Western grebes stage amazing displays to attract mates. One of the most dramatic courtship displays

These Western grebes were caught in action! They are performing a courtship display known as rushing.

is known as *rushing*. Rushing begins when a western grebe, looking for a mate, calls out loudly: *"Cree creet! Cree creet! Cree creet!"* Answering cries bounce back and forth across the water. Swimming slowly toward each other, two grebes are soon face to face.

Each bird stares hard at the other. With its head low and its throat bulging, each grebe points its bill and calls with harsh, machine-gunlike sounds. Eventually, one bird dips its head in the water, and then jerks it up toward the sky, shaking it back and forth furiously. Then, the grebe lowers its head again, stares, and calls harshly.

Suddenly, whirling to one side, the grebes lunge out of the water. Together they rush across the water, bodies upright, heads forward. They hold their folded wings stiffly out on either side of their bodies. Their feet slap the water furiously and rapidly. At the end of a 16- to 66-foot (5- to 20-m) rush, the birds dive headfirst into the water.

The grebes' rush across the water is powered by their feet. Unlike the foot of a duck, the foot of the western grebe is not webbed. Grebes have lobed feet instead. Folds of skin hang down from three long front toes. In the water, these folds flatten out, so that a small foot suddenly becomes a big foot.

The feet of the grebe move rapidly across the surface of the water. One scientist timed the grebe's movement at sixteen to twenty steps per second. Those fast-moving feet create a strong force in the water. As they churn up the suface, water is pushed down and back. The resulting drag force helps support the grebe and push it forward.

The grebe's wings may also help support the bird as it rushes across the water's surface. Some scientists believe the wings act as an *airfoil*, catching the air in a way that

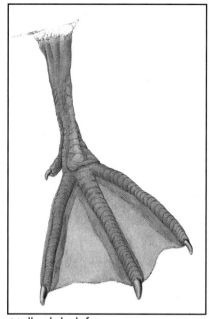

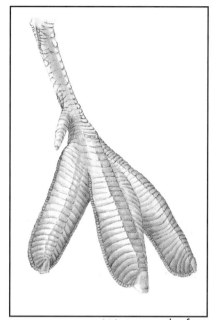

Mallard duck foot

Western grebe foot

While ducks have webbed feet to help them swim, grebes have lobed feet. In the water, the lobes flatten out, allowing grebes to rush along the water's surface.

lifts the bird's body upward. But, most scientists believe the feet support most of the bird's weight as it moves across the water.

The grebe also uses its feet to move underwater. When a grebe is hunting for fish, it floats along the surface and looks into the water below. Sometimes the grebe even sticks its face underwater. As soon as the bird spies a fish, it plunges straight down. Both feet kick together to push it down through the water. The grebe stabs the fish with its spearlike bill and returns to the surface a few moments later.

The western grebe usually hunts and feeds alone. Mating pairs, however, hunt together just before the female lays her eggs. During this time, the female grebe nags her

Western grebes are skillful, ferocious hunters.

This mating pair is putting the finishing touches on their nest, using mud and plant material brought up from the lake bottom.

mate to feed her with low clucking sounds. After a successful dive, the male grebe passes his catch to his partner. The mating grebes build a nest together, and, as spring turns into summer, they raise a small brood of two or three chicks.

Western grebes remain on the water throughout the summer. As the days begin to grow shorter and cooler, the birds instinctively know that it is time to migrate. One night, without warning, the grebes take to the air.

Grebes fly only at night. During the day, they rest and feed at small lakes. When they reach the Pacific coast, they search for their home wintering grounds. There they stay until spring returns.

CHAPTER FOUR

An Eight-Legged Fisherman: The Fisher Spider

A large brown spider with white racing stripes and a sprinkling of white flecks and spots on its body sits quietly on a leaf. Its eight eyes stare at the silvery web on which its front legs rest. The web trembles as a small insect lands on it. The insect struggles, but cannot free itself. Leaping up, the spider rushes to capture its *prey*. The spider seizes the small insect and injects poison with its strong fangs. A few moments later, the insect becomes still, and the spider carries its kill back to the leaf.

This is no ordinary spider and no ordinary web. This is *Dolomedes triton*, one type of fisher spider. It is common on the banks of ponds as well as in ditches and swamps. The fisher spider is unusual because it

As it waits for a victim, a fisher spider often rests part of its body on floating leaves. The spider always keeps a few legs on the surface film, so it can detect approaching prey.

doesn't spin its own web, and its web is unusual because it is not made of thin silk fibers. It is made of water molecules. The web of Dolomedes is water's invisible skin, the surface film.

How does the fisher spider keep from becoming a victim of this watery web? Its body and legs are clothed in a special waterproof coat—a layer of short hairs. The hairs are close together, making it hard for water to soak in.

The hairs on the legs and body of this large fisher spider repel water.

To test this idea, try the following activity. Using a medicine dropper, place a drop of water on a piece of *velvet*. Place another drop on a piece of cotton cloth. Look at each drop after 1 minute, 5 minutes, and 60 minutes.

What did you see? By 5 minutes, the water drop had probably soaked into the cotton material. But, it was still sitting on top of the velvet. Even after 60 minutes, that drop of water was still on the velvet!

Why? A drop of water is covered by an invisible skin or film. The threads of the cotton cloth tug at the water molecules along the drop's surface. Soon, the surface skin breaks apart. Water pours out, wetting the cotton cloth.

Why does the velvet remain dry? The air trapped in the hairs of the velvet pushes away the surface water molecules, so the water's surface skin remains intact. The tiny hairs that make up velvet act like the hairy coat of the fisher spider. Both repel water.

Some very small creatures need only a waterproof covering to stay on top of the surface film. Larger, heavier animals like the fisher spider depend on other special adaptations, too. To keep from falling through the surface film, the fisher spider stands and moves on water in an unusual way.

Do your parents sometimes tell you to stand up straight? If you were a young fisher spider, they might tell you just the opposite! The fisher spider slouches and sprawls across the water's surface. All of its body and most of its

long legs rest on the surface film. If the spider stood up, so that only the ends of its legs touched the water, the surface film would tear, sending the fisher spider into the water. But, the spider's sprawling posture spreads its weight out over a larger surface area, so the amount of weight supported by any given point on the water's surface is not too great.

A fisher spider slouches and sprawls its long legs so it won't fall through the water's surface.

This fisher spider has ducked underwater for a bit. The silvery sheen of its legs and body is due to the air trapped in its coat. To rise to the surface, the spider will simply release its grip on the plant stem.

In the wild, Dolomedes seldom falls through the surface film by accident. When frightened, however, it sometimes dives underwater to hide. Once below the surface, a silvery bubble forms around the spider. Then, buoyed by the air trapped in its hairy coat, the fisher spider rises readily to the surface.

To move across the water's surface, the fisher spider swings its middle pairs of legs back and forth like the oars of a rowboat. First the third pair, then the second pair, press against the water's surface. With each push, the animal glides forward. Its back legs trail behind and, like the rudder on a sailboat, help the spider steer.

At least one kind of fisher spider also runs or gallops across the water. *Dolomedes plantarius* runs five times faster than it rows. When the spider lands on the water's surface at the end of each stride, all eight legs, but no part of its body, touch the water. The spider gains *momentum* for its next leap forward by pushing off from the water's surface each time it lands.

As *D. plantarius* runs, it spins a "safety thread." The spider anchors one end of its safety line to the bank and holds the other end with one of its legs. After galloping across the water's slippery surface, the spider pinches down on the safety line and skids to a halt. Without that line, this fisher spider would slide right past its victim.

All fisher spiders are *predators*. But not all of their victims are insects trapped on the water's surface. The fisher spider gets its name from its ability to catch small fish. In fact, this spider can prey on fish that are two or three times its size.

To lure a fish, the fisher spider jiggles the water's surface with the tip of one leg. A small fish, intrigued by the

A fisher spider feeds on one of its favorite meals—a small fish.

movement above it, swims to the surface. When the fish is within the fisher spider's grasp, the spider reaches down into the water and grabs the prey with its strong front legs. The spider sinks its fangs into the flesh at the base of the fish's head and clings tightly as its victim thrashes wildly in the water. Venom flows from the spider's fangs into the fish's body. Within minutes, the victim goes limp.

So, you see, Dolomedes is anything but an ordinary spider. It is a water walker, a skilled fisher, and the largest of all the creatures that move on the water's surface film.

Water striders on the surface of a shallow pond in Grand Teton National Park in northwestern Wyoming.

CHAPTER FIVE

SKATERS WITH A DEADLY MISSION: THE WATER STRIDER

Would you like to see some animals that walk on water for yourself? Your best bet might be to look for water striders. Watch for long-legged insects with dark narrow bodies. They live on quiet ponds and slow-moving streams all over the world.

Water striders often gather in large groups on the quiet, shady waters of streams and ponds. As they glide effortlessly over the surface of the water, they look as graceful as figure skaters practicing in a crowded ice rink.

Water striders spend most of their lives on the water's surface. There they feed, grow into adults, find mates, and lay eggs. Water striders retreat to the bank and hide among the plants and rocks only when rain ripples the surface or cold temperatures cause the water to freeze.

A young water strider feeds on a fly. The strider's beak has pierced the prey's *exoskeleton* to inject digestive *enzymes*.

Although the water strider's movements appear peaceful and serene, this animal is actually a fierce predator. Like the fisher spider, its hunting ground is the water's surface. Its victims are the small insects that become trapped in the surface film. When the prey struggles to free itself, it creates ripples in the water. Water striders can sense these tiny waves and use them to locate prey.

With a cat-like pounce, water striders grab struggling insects with their front legs. They quickly stab the prey with their sharp beaks and inject *saliva* into the victim's body. Within minutes, the saliva turns the prey's body tissues into a liquid. The vampirelike strider then sucks up all the juices, leaving only a shrunken, dry husk.

In its search for prey, the water strider darts and glides easily on the water. This insect's long middle and hind legs spread outward from its body. These legs support the body,

A water strider's legs support it's body, so that it can stand on and move across the water's surface.

so that it never touches the water's surface. The strider's short front legs, which it holds up under its head, are used to grab and hold prey.

The strider spreads part of its middle legs and much of its long back legs over the water's surface. As a result, its body weight is supported over a large surface area. If the water strider placed too much of its weight on a small surface area, it might fall through the surface of the water. Humans use snowshoes for the same reason. We are less likely to sink into soft, fresh snow if our body weight is spread out over a larger surface area.

To move along the water's surface, the water strider pushes its long middle legs against the surface film. Both middle legs move together like the oars of a rowboat. Each push is followed by a glide along the water's slippery surface. The strider uses its hind legs to steer.

How do water striders travel across the surface film? What makes them different from other insects? The answer has something to do with the tiny hairs that cover the water strider's body and legs.

These hairs repel water. A water strider combs its hair often. The strider uses its built-in combs to remove dust particles, keep the hairs in line, and spread a thin coating of oil over the hairs. Grooming keeps the water strider's hairy coat water-repellent.

As the strider presses against the surface film, the *buoyant force* of the water pushes upward. The water strider's

Each pair of this water strider's legs has a different function. The long middle pair pushes the insect across the water, the back pair acts as rudders for steering, and the front pair grasps prey during feeding.

coat of tiny hairs traps air, giving the animal some *buoyancy*. While the surface film supports most of the strider's weight, the water's upward push provides some additional support.

Sometimes water striders do fall through the surface film. They may be pushed under by the rush of water in a small current, or a heavy rain may soak the insect, sending it below the surface of the water. Water rolls off the body of a young healthy water strider, and it bobs back up to the surface. After its hairs dry, the strider is able to move across the water's surface again.

As they grow older, though, water striders lose their water-repellent covering. The hairs begin to break off or fall out. As a result, the hairs become wet and the striders have trouble staying on the surface of the water. If they fall through the surface film, they drown.

It's not only their velvety coat and special legs that set these insects apart from others. Water striders also have a unique way of communicating with one another. They transmit messages over the water's surface film.

How do they do this? Throw a small stone into a body of water and watch the ripples spread out over the water's surface. These ripples are like the messages that water striders send and receive.

They create messages by drumming on the water. Male striders beat the water's surface when they have found a good site for mating. Female striders sometimes signal in

Courting water striders like this mating pair talk to one another using tiny surface waves. Rapid up-and-down movements of their front legs generate these surface ripples.

return. Male striders also send signals that warn other males to stay away. This is how they defend their territories and protect their mates during egg-laying.

Indian scouts on the American frontier put an ear to the ground to listen for the pounding of horses' hooves. Water striders use their feet to feel the ripples on the water's surface. Special nerve cells in their leg joints sense these small waves.

Sit on the bank of a pond for a while and keep an eye on the water's surface. Can you see the water strider's ripple talk? Watch the striders as they gracefully glide across the surface. Enjoy your free ticket to nature's skating party!

CHAPTER SIX

An Aquatic Pedestrian: The Water Measurer

Water striders row—and sometimes hop—on the water's surface. What they don't do is simply walk. Where can you find an animal that actually *walks* on water? Are there any such creatures?

Yes, there are. Just look for a pond with lots of floating plants and algae. If you are lucky, you will see a tiny insect walking slowly over the surface. This pale creature is a water measurer.

Through a magnifying glass, this water walker looks like a walkingstick, a common forest insect. Without a magnifying glass, a water measurer is hard to see. The water measurer is less than 1/2 inch (1 cm) long from head to tail—not much bigger than a splinter of wood stuck in your finger.

Like the walkingstick, the body of this water bug is long and narrow. Even its head is long and narrow.

This water measurer is walking across a mat of algae with a recently captured meal.

In fact, its head is as long as its *thorax*, or middle body segment. Halfway down either side of the insect's head sit two small eyes. Two long jointed *antennae* project forward from the front of its head. The water measurer's spear-shaped beak is hidden underneath its head.

Three pairs of stilt-like legs hold the insect above the surface of the pond, so that its body never touches the water. The water measurer's legs are long and slender like very thin hairs.

The water measurer walks on six legs. Unlike its relative the water strider, the water measurer places only its small feet and claws on the water. Each leg moves independently from the leg on the opposite side. With its long limbs, this insect has little trouble walking on top of the floating plants and algae.

But, when a water measurer crosses an area of open water, it moves carefully. Its feet press into the surface film, creating tiny dimples. A dense covering of velvety hairs protects its feet from the water below. The water measurer is named for its slow, deliberate movement.

A tiny claw at the tip of each foot pokes into the surface film. Although the water measurer's feet are waterproof, its claws are not. However, the claws do not tear the water's surface because most of the animal's weight is carried by the back of its feet.

As the water measurer steps carefully on the pond's surface, its long antennae wave from side to side and its

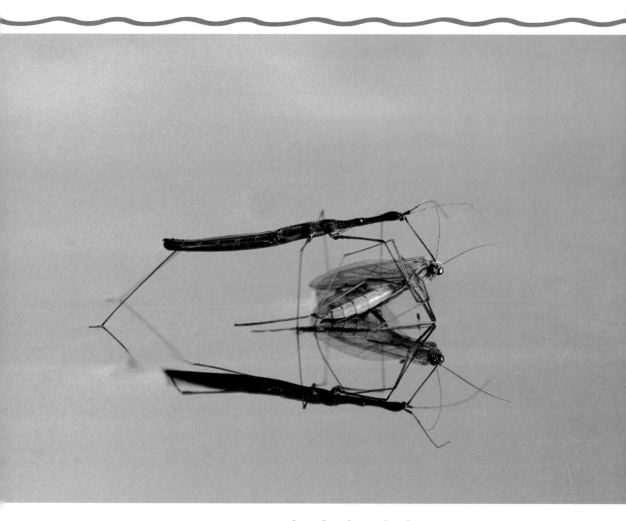

A water measurer stabs the head of its prey with its long spear-shaped beak.

head bobs. Suddenly, the water measurer stiffens. It has spotted a dying insect in its path. The cautious hunter slowly draws near. When it reaches the struggling insect, the water measurer bends its antennae down until they come into contact with its prey. In one quick motion, the water measurer lowers its beak, thrusts its deadly mouthpart forward, and spears its prey. Tiny hooks or barbs on the insect's beak hold the prey in place.

When the victim stops struggling, the water measurer lifts its beak clear of the water's surface and carries its prey to a nearby mat of floating algae. Its footing now secure, the hunter eats its prey. Hidden mouthparts rasp and file the soft body parts of the victim. The water measurer's saliva turns the tissues into a juicy fluid. The water measurer then sucks up the fluid, and, within minutes, the victim's body crumples to a shapeless form.

Rove beetles live in many different habitats.
This rove beetle lives among the leaf litter on the
forest floor.

CHAPTER SEVEN

Jet Skier: The Rove Beetle

S*tenus bipunctatus* is one type of rove beetle. Although it is found in most parts of the world, it is not well known. If you saw one, you probably wouldn't even think it was a beetle. It looks very different from a Junebug (June beetle) or ladybug (ladybird beetle). Stenus is about the same size as a grain of rice, and looks more like a tiny black wasp. Its short wings only partly cover its long, pointed *abdomen*, and its large eyes peer out of a round, ant-like head.

Rove beetles live in almost every kind of *habitat*. You can find them in flowers, on mushrooms, or under fallen leaves on the forest floor. Some live in the bodies of dead animals. Others live in ant colonies. Stenus prefers damp places near ponds and streams, where it spends its time hunting small insects—especially a tiny wingless insect called a springtail.

It is a sunny summer afternoon, and a Stenus is stalking a springtail, which is about the size of a grain of ground black pepper. As the hunter moves across the stream bank, its antennae are pointed forward, and its abdomen curls upward. Stenus leans forward slightly as it closes in on its prey. Zap! The beetle shoots a tiny harpoonlike structure out of its mouth. Bull's-eye! The sharp tip of this expandable mouthpart lodges itself deep within the springtail's body. The rove beetle quickly draws its prey back into its mouth.

Using its cutting mouthparts, Stenus cuts through the springtail's outer covering or exoskeleton. The rove beetle then vomits into the wound. Enzymes in the fluid vomited by Stenus break down the prey's soft body parts. Within minutes, the body tissues turn to soup and dinner is ready. Stenus laps it up.

But, this rove beetle doesn't always catch its prey. Chasing a springtail along a stream bank can be dangerous. Sometimes Stenus falls and ends up on the water's surface. Unable to swim, the beetle could drown or be eaten by predators. But Stenus has a way to avoid these dangers.

When it does fall onto the surface of the water, Stenus moves quickly back to the bank. It doesn't use its legs. It doesn't walk, run, jump, or row. Yet it can zip across the surface at an amazing 30 inches (76 cm) per second.

When it hits the water, Stenus points the tip of its abdomen downward and squirts an oily substance out of

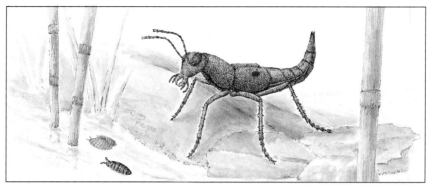

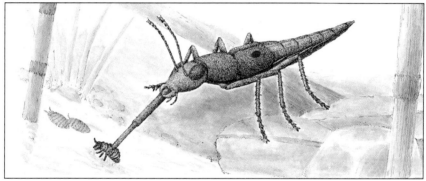

When a *Stenus bipunctatus* spots a potential meal, it shoots a tiny harpoonlike structure out of its mouth and stabs its victim.

its rear end. In a flash, the rove beetle jets across the water's surface. The beetle holds its front feet out like skis, and its hind legs trail behind. Its bent abdomen acts as a rudder, allowing Stenus to steer its way back to the bank.

With a little bit of liquid soap and some pepper grains, you too can make small objects skim rapidly across the water. Begin by pouring some water into a shallow bowl. Lightly sprinkle pepper evenly over the surface of the water. Now squeeze a little dishwashing soap onto the tip of your finger and touch one edge of the water's surface with that finger. You will see the pepper grains race across to the opposite side!

What has happened? Water molecules on the surface cling very tightly to their neighbors. They pull on each other, creating a force or tension like that in a stretched rubber band. This pulling force at the water's surface is called *surface tension.*

The dishwashing soap reduces the surface tension by preventing water molecules from pulling on each other. In the absence of this pulling force, the water molecules spread across the surface. When you touched the surface of the water with your soapy fingertip, the water molecules moved apart rapidly. This spreading force pushed the pepper grains quickly to the opposite side of the bowl.

The oily substance released by Stenus also creates a spreading force across the water's surface. That force pushes the rove beetle forward. A patch of dense hairs between the insect's middle pair of legs helps to waterproof it. The air trapped among the hairs gives the animal some buoyancy.

The water surface can be many things to different animals. To the water strider, it's a place to hunt for food, and a place to walk, run, or even jump. The basilisk lizard uses it to escape from enemies. But, to the little rove beetle, the water surface is a dangerous place, a place to avoid. Safety lies on the stream bank, and jet skiing is its ticket home.

GLOSSARY

abdomen—in insects, the third or last body section. It includes the heart, stomach, intestines, and reproductive organs.

airfoil—a structure, such as a wing, designed to help lift or control an aircraft as it flies.

antenne (plural *antennae*)—a slender feeler located on the head of an insect. It contains sense organs.

buoyancy—the tendency of a body to float or rise when submerged in a fluid.

buoyant—having the quality or property of buoyancy.

buoyant force—the upward force exerted by a fluid upon a body placed in it.

displace—to crowd out, take the place of; to put (an object) in place of another.

drag force—the force put out by a liquid on an object moving through it.

enzyme—a substance produced by living cells that can cause a specific chemical reaction to occur. Examples include the substances produced by the stomach and small intestines that aid in the digestion of food.

exoskeleton—an animal's outer skeleton or supportive covering.

force—a push or a pull.

habitat—the place where a plant, animal, or other living thing naturally lives and grows.

Middle Ages—the period of European history extending from A.D. 500 to 1500. This period is known for its castles and knights in armor.

molecule—the smallest physical unit of a substance that can exist and retain its chemical properties.

momentum—a property of a moving body that is determined by multiplying its mass and its velocity.

Newton's third law of motion—one of three laws that describe the motion of matter. According to this law, whenever one force pushes or pulls an object, another force pushes or pulls the same object in the opposite direction.

predator—an animal that kills and eats other animals.

prey—an animal that is hunted and killed by other animals for food.

rushing—a courtship display of the western grebe.

saliva—a watery fluid secreted into the mouth by the salivary glands. It assists in the digestion of food.

surface film—the surface of a liquid such as water that acts like a stretched elastic membrane.

surface tension—a property of the surface of a liquid that makes the surface pull together to take up the smallest possible area. It is caused by the attraction of molecules in the liquid.

thorax—in insects, the middle or second body segment. It is located between the head and the abdomen, and the insect's legs and wings are attached to it.

tissue—a group of similar cells working together to perform a specific task. An organ consists of several tissues.

velvet—a fabric with a lawn of short dense threads that project upward from the surface of the material.

FOR FURTHER READING

Burnie, David. *Birds and How They Live*. New York: Dorling Kindersley, Inc., 1992.

Cooke, John A. L. *The Restless Kingdom*. New York: Facts on File, Inc., 1991.

Gunston, Bill. *Water*. Morristown, NJ: Silver Burdett Company, 1980.

Hadden, Sue. *Insects*. New York: Thomson Learning, 1993.

Howell, Catherine Herbert. *Reptiles and Amphibians*. Washington, DC: National Geographic Society, 1993.

Johnson, Jinny. *Simon & Schuster Children's Guide to Birds*. New York: Simon & Schuster Books for Young Readers, 1996.

Jones, D. *Spider, the Story of a Predator and its Prey.* New York: Facts on File Publications, 1986.

Kuhn, Dwight and David M. Schwartz. *The Hidden Life of the Pond.* New York: Crown Publishers, Inc., 1988.

Parker, Steve. *Pond & River.* New York: Alfred A. Knopf, 1988.

Patent, Dorothy Hinshaw. *Spider Magic.* New York: Holiday House, 1982.

Reid, George K. *Pond Life: Guide to Common Plants and Animals of North American Ponds and Lakes.* Racine, WI: Western Publishing Company, Inc., 1987.

Simon, Seymour. *Soap Bubble Magic.* New York: Lothrop, Lee & Shepard Books, 1985.

Smith, Trevor. *Amazing Lizards.* New York: Alfred A. Knopf, 1990.

Taylor, Barbara. *Liquid and Buoyancy.* New York: Warwick Press, 1990.

Ward, Alan. *Experimenting with Surface Tension and Bubbles.* London: Dryad Press Limited, 1985.

INDEX

Airfoil, 22–23
Antennae, 47, 49

Basilisk lizard, *12*, 13–19, 55
   feet, 18–19, *18*
   head crest, 13, *15*
   how it got its name,
     13–14, *14*
   how it moves, 9, 13,
     15–19, *17*, *18*
   size of, 15
Buoyancy, 10, 32, 42, 55
Buoyant force, 40

Displace water, 18–19
Dolomedes plantarius, 33
Dolomedes triton. See
   Fisher spider

Drag force, 10, 18, 19, 22
Dragons, 13–14, *14*
Drumming, 42–44, *43*
Duck, 22, 23

Enzymes, 38, 52
Exoskeleton, 38, 52
Experiments and activities
   experience drag force, 10
   observe surface film, 11
   repel water, 30
   surface tension, 54

Feet, 18–19, *18*, 22–24, *23*
Film, 9, 10–11, 39–42, *39*,
   41, 45. *See also* Walking
   a trap, 27–29, *28*, 38
Fisher spider, 27–35

hiding underwater, 32
how it moves, 30–31, *31*, 33
hunting, 27–29, *28*,
  33–35, *34*
waterproof coat, *29*
Force, 9–10, 54. *See also*
  Drag force

Galloping, 33
Grebes. *See* Western grebe
Grooming, 40

Habitat
  basilisk lizard, 15
  Fisher spider, 27
  rove beetle, 50, 51
  water measurer, 45
  water strider, 37
  western grebe, 20
Hair, waterproof coat, 30
  of fisher spider, 29
  of rove beetle, 55
  of water measurer, 47
  of water strider, 40, 42
Hiding underwater, 32
Hopping, 45

Jesus Christ lizard, 16

Jetting, 52, 54–55

King of serpents, *14*

Mallard duck, 23
Mating and courtship
  basilisk lizard, *15*
  water striders, 42–44, *43*
  western grebe, 20–22, *21*,
    24–25, *25*
Middle Ages, 13–14, *14*
Migration, 20, 26
Molecules, 10, 30, 54
Momentum, 33

Newton, Isaac, 16
Newton's third law of motion,
  16

Predator, 33, 38

Rove beetles, *50*, 51–55
  how it moves, 52, 54–55
  hunting, 52, *53*
  size, 51
Rowing, 33, 40, 45
Running, 9, 13, 15–19, *17*,
  33, 54

Rushing, 20–22, *21*

Safety thread, 33
Saliva, 39, 49
Skin. *See* Film
Speed
  of basilisk lizard, 19
  and drag force, 19
  of rove beetle, 52
  of western grebe, 22
Spiders, 10. *See* Fisher spider
Springtail, 51–52
Surface film. *See* Film
Surface tension, 54
Stenus bipunctatus, *53*. *See also* Rove beetles
Swimming, 19, 21

Thorax, 47
Tissues
  and buoyancy, 10
  turn to liquid, 39, 49, 54

Velvet, 30
Venom, 27, 35

Walking, 9, 45, 46, 47–49, *48*

Water dancer. *See* Western grebe
Water measurer, 45–49
  how it moves, 45, *46*, 47–49, *48*
  and prey, 46, 47, 48, 49
  size, 45
Waterproof. *See* Hair
Water strider, 9, 36, 37–44
  age and drowning, 42
  communication, 42–44, *43*
  how it moves, 39–42, *39*, *41*, 45
  hunting, 38–39, *38*
  resting, 8
Web, 27–29, *28*
Western Grebe, 10, 20–26
  feet, 22–24, *23*
  how they hunt, 23–24, *24*
  mating pairs, 24–25, *25*
  migration, 20, 26
  rushing, 20–22, *21*
  when they fly, 26
  wings, 22–23
Wings, as airfoil, 22–23

About the Author

Patricia A. Fink Martin brings to children's literature the breadth and depth of knowledge of a professional biologist with the ability to communicate and the enthusiasm of an educator. She is a graduate of the University of Missouri. Continuing her training at Michigan State University, she received an M.S. in biochemistry. After teaching at a junior college for 2 years, Dr. Martin attended Idaho State University and completed a doctorate in the biological sciences with an emphasis on biology education.

Dr. Martin spent a number of years teaching college-level biochemistry, cell biology, anatomy, botany, zoology, and evolution. While teaching at a liberal arts college, she received a National Science Foundation award that allowed her to collaborate with a researcher at a nearby medical school.

Since moving to Florida, Dr. Martin has tutored a home-schooled first-grader in science and participated in a national pen-pal program designed to bring young students in touch with a professional scientist.